THE REED
NEW ZEALAND
PICTURE
DICTIONARY

Established in 1907, Reed Publishing (NZ) Ltd
is New Zealand's largest book publisher, with over 300 titles in print.

For details on all these books visit our website:

www.reed.co.nz

Published by Reed Books, a division of Reed Publishing (NZ) Ltd,
39 Rawene Rd, Birkenhead, Auckland 10. Associated companies,
branches and representatives throughout the world.

© 2002 Reed Publishing (NZ) Ltd
The authors assert their moral rights in the work.
Illustrations by Dale Tutill

ISBN 1 86948 786 9
First published 2001 as *The Reed Maori Picture Dictionary*
by Margaret Sinclair and Ross Calman
This edition first published 2002

Printed in New Zealand

THE REED
NEW ZEALAND
PICTURE
DICTIONARY

REED

Contents

Aa

above

My hut is **above** the ground.

accident

action song

address
I wrote the **address** on the envelope.

adult

An **adult** helped me to cross the road.

aerobics

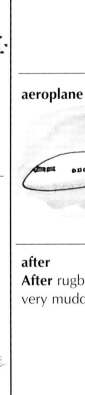

aeroplane

after
After rugby I am very muddy.

afternoon
This **afternoon** I walked home from school.

air
The paper dart flew through the **air**.

airport

alarm clock

albatross

all

He ate **all** my chocolates!

A
a

alligator

ambulance

ancestor

My **ancestor** signed the Treaty.

anchor

angel

angry

Sometimes my little brother makes me **angry**.

animal
Which one is your favourite **animal**?

ankle

answer
Some of the questions are difficult to **answer**.

answerphone

ant

anxious
If I get home late, Mum is **anxious**.

apple

apple juice

apron

arm

arrow

artist

ashamed

I am **ashamed** of my old shoes.

assembly

I sang at **assembly**.

astronaut

athlete

auntie
My **auntie** gave me a great birthday present.

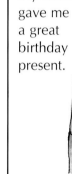

autumn

axe

Bb

baby
babysitter

back
backpack

bacon

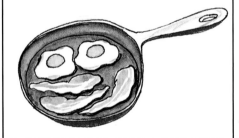

bad
Bad dog!

badge

bag

bait
Dad cut up
the **bait.**

bakery
I like to buy
cakes from
our local
bakery.

bald

ball

ballet

balloon

banana

bandage

bank

I am fishing from the **bank** of
the river.

bank

I put my money in the **bank** for
safekeeping.

barbecue

bare

I like having **bare** feet.

bark

basket

basketball

bat

bath
bathroom

I like to have a **bath** in our **bathroom**.

beach

beak

beard

beat
I love to **beat** the drum.

beautiful

My mother is **beautiful**.

bed

bedroom
bedtime

I have to go to my **bedroom** when it is **bedtime**.

bee

beef

beehive

before
I put on my helmet **before** I ride my bike.

B b

bell

bellbird

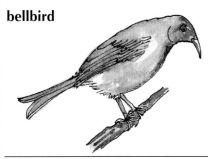

below
The plates are **below** the cups.

belt

berry

beside
The river runs **beside** our school.

between

I like to sleep **between** Mum and Dad.

bicycle

big

bird

birthday
It's my **birthday**.

biscuit

black

blackberry

blackboard

blanket

blind

blood
There was **blood** on my knee after I fell over.

blow
The wind will **blow** my balloon away.

blow
I can **blow** my nose.

blue

boat

body
Healthy food will make my **body** strong.

bone
That dog has a big **bone** in its mouth!

book

boot

bottle

bouncy castle

bow
I can tie a **bow** in my shoelace.

bow

The **bow** of a canoe is at the front.

bowl
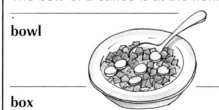

box

boy
Aidan is a **boy**.

bracelet

branch

brave
Be **brave**!

BEWARE OF DOG

bread

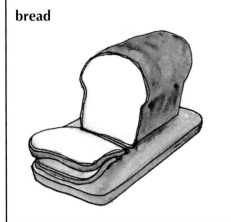

breakfast

breath

I hold my **breath** under water.

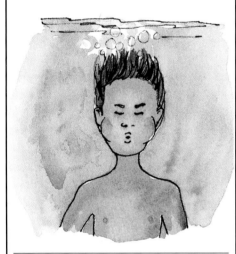

breeze

The **breeze** lifts my kite.

bride
bridegroom

bridge

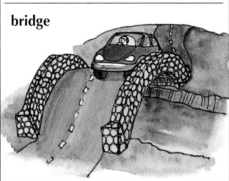

broken

broom

brother

Tama is Marama's **brother**.

brown

bubbles

bucket

budgie

buggy

builder

bull

bulldozer

bumblebee

burglar
burglar alarm

bus
bus driver
bus stop

bush

I love to walk through the **bush**.

butter

butterfly

button

9

Cc

cabbage
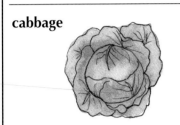

cabbage tree

café

Mum and I went to the **café** for lunch.

cage

cake

calculator

calendar

calf

call

I **call** for my mum when I have a nightmare.

camera

camp

canoe

cap

car

card
I made a **card** for Father's Day.

carpark

carpet
I spilled juice on the **carpet**.

carrot

cartoons

I like the **cartoons** best.

cassette

castle

cat

catch

caterpillar

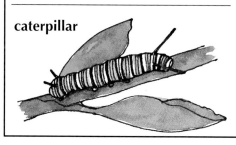

cauliflower

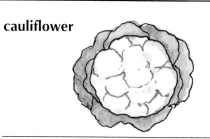

cave

cellphone

cemetery

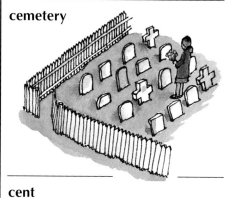

cent

The five-**cent** piece is smaller than the ten-**cent** piece.

cereal

certificate

I got a **certificate** for excellent writing.

chain

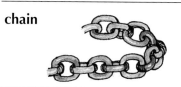

chair

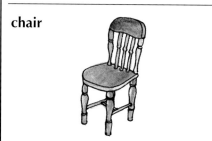

challenge

The **challenge** is the first part of a Māori welcome.

champion

I am the **champion** at marbles.

chase

We like to **chase** the seagulls at the beach.

cheek

cheese

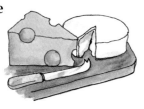

chemist

chest

Tarzan beats his **chest**.

chicken

I love to eat roasted **chicken**.

chicks

chief

child

children

chin

chips

chocolate

Christmas

church

cicada

circus

city
I live in a
big **city**.

clap

class
classroom

claw

cliff

climb

cloak
A **cloak** will keep
you warm.

clock

clothes

clothes dryer

cloud

clown

coat

coffee

cold
It's too **cold** for swimming.

cold
I've got a bad **cold**.

colour
Green is
my favourite
colour.

comb

come
Mum calls, '**Come** in for dinner!'

comic book

committee

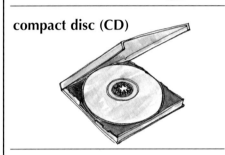

compact disc (CD)

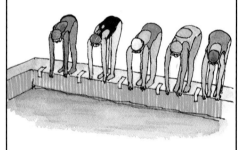

competition
competitor

I am a **competitor** in the interschool swimming **competition**.

computer
computer game

the cook
to cook

The cook agreed **to cook** the meals.

corn

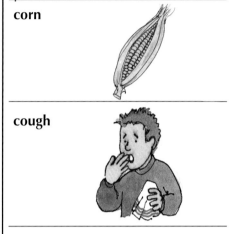

cough

council

count

One, two, three, four, five.

My little brother can **count** to five.

country

Australia is the closest **country** to New Zealand.

cousin

We went to our **cousin** Whetu's birthday party.

cow

crab

crane

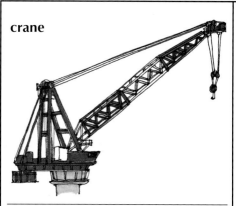

crash

crayfish

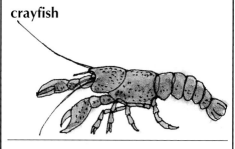

crayon

cream
I like whipped **cream** on my cake.

creek

cricket

cricket

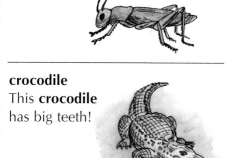

crocodile
This **crocodile** has big teeth!

crowd

crown

cry

cuddle

culture

I am learning about Māori **culture** at school.

cup

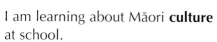

cupboard

curtain

customer
The **customer** was served by the shop owner.

Dd

dad

daffodil

dairy

daisy

damp
My shorts were **damp** after I sat on the grass.

dance

dancer

date

daughter

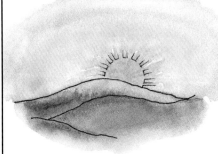

dawn
day
The **dawn** has brought another sunny **day**!

dead

decorate

We **decorate** the room for my party.

decoration

delicious

dentist

desert

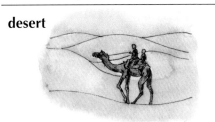

desk

destroy

detective

diamond

dictionary

I look up hard words in the **dictionary**.

die

dig

digger

dinghy

I can row the **dinghy**.

dinner

dinosaur

dirty

dishes

dishwasher

disk

disobedient

dive

D d

diver

doctor

dog
The **dog** looks happy!

doll

dollar

dolphin

donkey

door
I hid behind the **door**.

doughnut

dragon

dragonfly

drawing

dream

dress
Kerry is wearing a pretty **dress**.

dress
I can **dress** myself.

dressing gown

drill

drink

driver
driving

The racing **driver** loves **driving** very fast.

drown

Don't swim there or you might **drown**.

duck

Ee

ear
earring

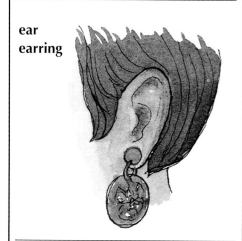

Earth

earthquake

If there is an **earthquake** I will get under a table.

Easter
Easter egg

At **Easter** we had an **Easter egg** hunt.

eat

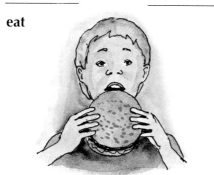

eel

egg
eggcup

elbow

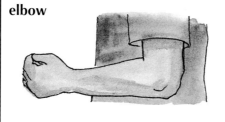

election

There is an **election** every three years to decide our government.

electricity

Electricity makes our lights work.

elephant

elf

e-mail

I sent an **e-mail** to my friend in Australia.

E e

embarrassed

I feel **embarrassed** when I sing in front of the class.

emergency

Dial 111 if there is an **emergency**.

emotions

Happiness and sadness are two **emotions**.

empty

enemy

engine

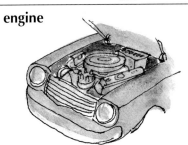

envelope

Miss Sue Smith
10 Leafy Lane
Greenville.

escalator

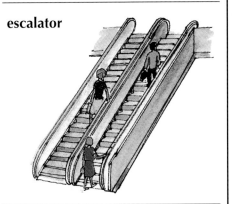

excited

I am very **excited** about our trip today.

exercise

explode

explore

I want to **explore** the jungle.

eye
eyebrow

Ff

face

I wash my **face**.

factory

fairy

family

famous

The All Blacks are **famous**.

fantail

farm
farmer

My uncle owns a **farm**. He is a good **farmer**.

fast

I can run very **fast**.

father

Father Christmas

fear

I have a **fear** of spiders!

feast

feather

fed up

I get **fed up** when Mum chats for too long.

F f

feed

I like to **feed** the lamb.

feelings

It hurts my **feelings** if people call me names.

feet

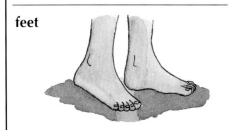

felt-tip pen

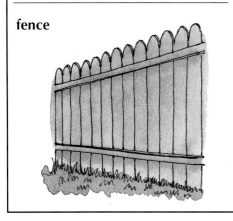

fence

few

There are only a **few** peas left.

fierce

field

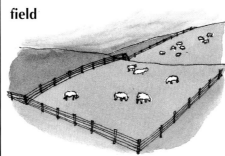

fight

find

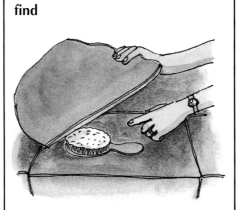

Mum helps me **find** my hairbrush.

finger

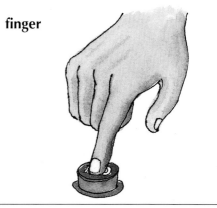

finished

I have **finished** my book.

fire

fire engine
fire fighter

The **fire engine** is driven by a **fire fighter**.

firewood

fireworks

first aid

We have a **first aid** kit at home.

fish

fisherman
fishing rod

The **fisherman** dropped his
fishing rod.

fish-hook

fishing

I love to go **fishing**.

fist

flag

flax

float

flood

flounder

flour

flower

F f

flute

fly

fly

foam

There is **foam** at the bottom of the waterfall.

fog

Mum turns on the headlights in the **fog**.

fold

I help **fold** the washing.

food

foot
footprint

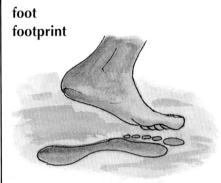

football

I play **football**.

forbidden

Fishing is **forbidden** in that river.

forehead

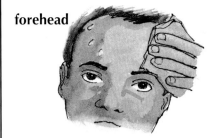

forest

There is a pine **forest** near our house.

fork

fort

fountain

freckles

freezer

French fries

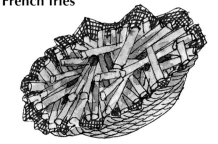

fridge

friend

frightened

The dog **frightened** me.

frog

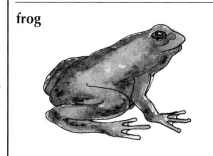

front

Our **front** door is red.

frost

Sometimes in winter there is **frost** on the leaves.

frown

My forehead wrinkles when I **frown**.

fruit

frying pan

funny

furniture

Gg

game

Hide and seek is my favourite **game**.

gang

We asked Kemo to join our **gang**.

garage
garage sale

garden
gate

gather

I help **gather** sticks for the fire.

gentle

I have to be **gentle** with the kitten.

germs

I wash my hands to get rid of any **germs**.

geyser

ghost

giant

gift

giraffe

girl

give

'**Give** me that book so I can **give** it to the librarian.'

glass

glasses

glow-worm

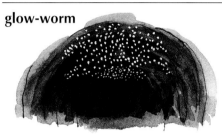

glue

go

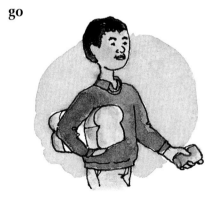

I **go** to the shop to get bread.

goat

goldfish

golf

good

I try to be **good**.
'Very **good**, well done!'
says my teacher.

goodbye

'**Goodbye**,' say Dad and Thomas.
'**Goodbye**,' say Mum and Rosie.

goose

gorilla

government

The **government** runs the country.

grandchild
grandfather
grandmother

grape

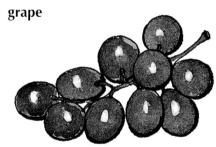

grapefruit

grapevine

grass

grasshopper

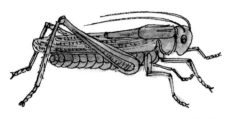

gravy

greedy

green

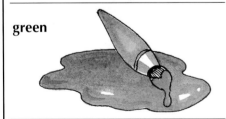

greenstone
This tiki is made of **greenstone**.

greet

grey

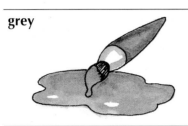

group

My **group** won the singing competition.

grow

We **grow** watercress at school.

grumble

Sometimes I **grumble** when I have to help Mum.

guests

The party **guests** arrived.

guide

guinea pig

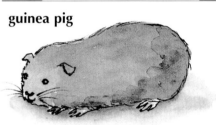

guitar

gun

gymnastics

Hh

hair
hairdresser

I get my **hair** cut by a **hairdresser**.

half

hall

School assembly is in the **hall**.

hamburger

hammer

hand

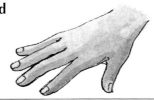

handbag

handle

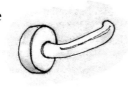

handsome

The girls all think Rangi is **handsome**.

hang-glider

happy

harbour

hard

My homework is very **hard**.

hard

Concrete is **hard**.

hat

hate

I **hate** being sick.

H
h

head
headphones

healthy

Exercise helps us stay **healthy**.

heart

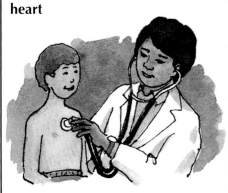

The doctor listens to my **heart** beating.

heater

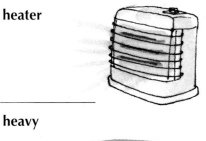

heavy

hedgehog

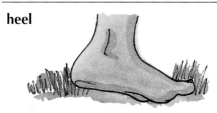

heel

helicopter

hello

Kia ora.

help

I **help** my dad water the garden.

hen

heron

hide

high school
My big sister
goes to **high
school**.

hill

hips

The leader says, 'Hands on **hips**!'

hippopotamus

hit
hockey

I hit the ball during our **hockey** game.

hold

I **hold** the cup of tea carefully.

hole

holiday

We are going on **holiday**.

home

Welcome **home**!

homework

honey

hook

horse

hospital

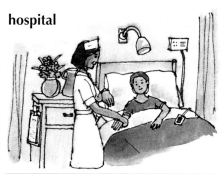

hot

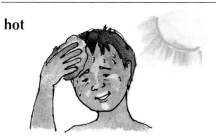

hot air balloon

hot dog

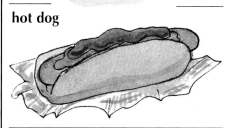

hotel

hour

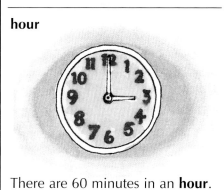

There are 60 minutes in an **hour**.

H h
I i

house

hug

hungry

husband

I pretend Sam is my **husband**.

hydroslide

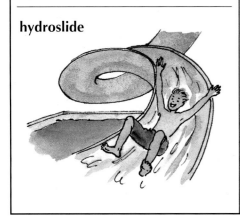

Ii

ice

ice cream

iceberg

icing

The cake has pink **icing**.

in

The dog is **in** the kennel.

injection

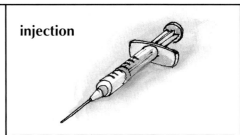

insect

inside

I have to stay **inside** because it is raining.

Internet

I found out lots about dinosaurs by using the **Internet**.

iron

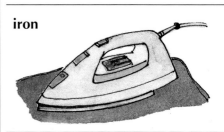

island

32

Jj

jacket

jail

jam jar

jealous

I am **jealous** of Sally. She won the race.

jeans

jelly

jellyfish
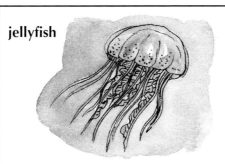

jewel

jewellery
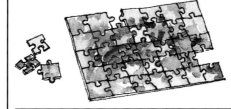

jigsaw puzzle

job

Mum gave me a **job** to do.

jogging

joke

Steve told me a good **joke**.

journey

We are going on a long **journey**.

judo

juice

jump

jumper

jungle

Kk

kangaroo
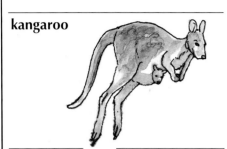

karate

kayak

kennel

kettle
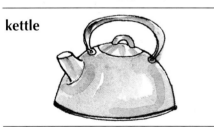

key
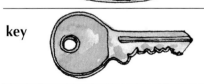

kick

kill

kindergarten

My little brother goes to **kindergarten**.

king

kingfisher

kiss

kitchen

kite
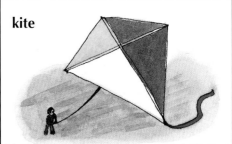

kitten

knee

kneel

knife

knot

know

I **know** they are talking about me.

koala

Ll

ladder

ladybird

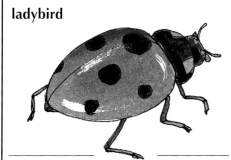

lake

lamb

land

landslide

language

Kei te pēhea koe?

I want to learn the Māori **language**.

laugh

lawnmower

lazy

leaf

leap

learn

I **learn** the recorder.

leave

I don't want to **leave**.

35

L l

leg

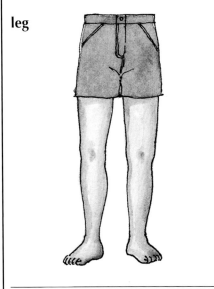

legend

The teacher told us the **legend** of Māui.

lemon

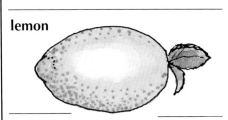

leopard

letter

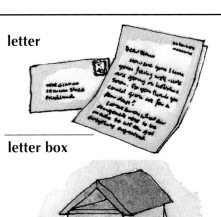

letter box

lettuce

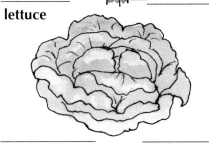

library

lick

lid

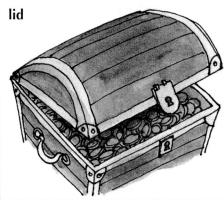

lie

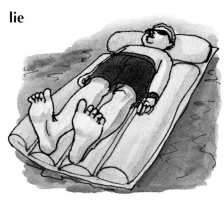

lift

light
I turn on the **light**.

light

As **light** as a feather.

lighthouse

lightning

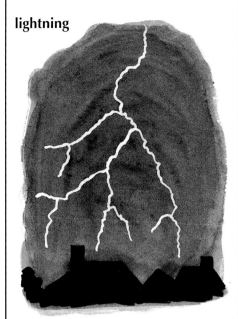

lion

lip
lipstick

listen

Mum says, '**Listen** to me.'

litter

I helped pick up **litter** from the playground.

little

lizard

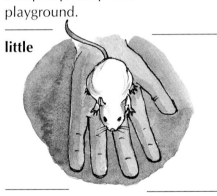

loaf

long

look

'**Look** at me,' says the teacher.

look!

love

lunch

Mm

magazine

magician

magnet

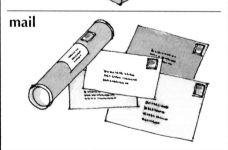

mail

make-up

man

mangrove

many

I have **many** marbles.

map

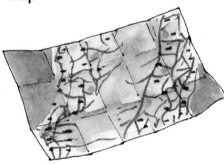

marry

mask

mat

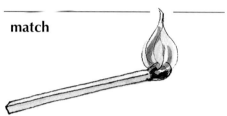

The cat sat on the **mat**.

match

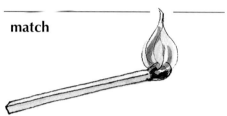

maths

meal

measles

measure

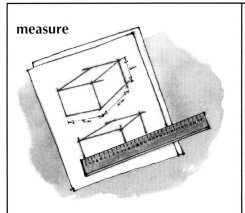

meat

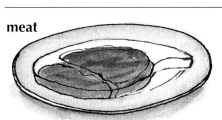

mechanic

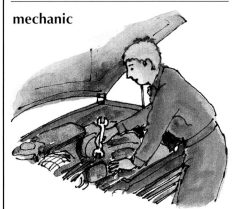

medal

medicine

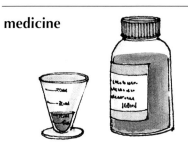

meet

melon

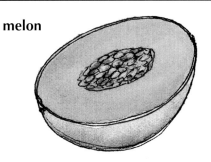

melt

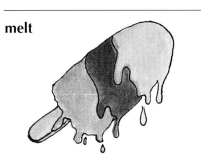

mend

I hope Mum can **mend** this.

merry-go-round

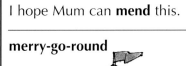

mess

message

I hand a **message** to the teacher.

messy

Painting is **messy** but fun.

microscope

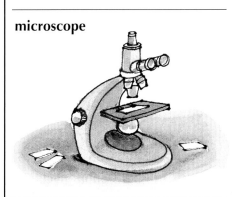

microwave

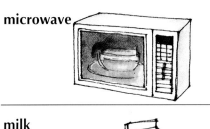

milk

minibus

mirror

M m

mischievous

My little sister is very **mischievous**.

miserable

miss

mist

The **mist** settles on the forest.

mistake

I made a **mistake** in my homework.

mix

money

monkey

monster

month

February is the shortest **month** in the year.

moon

morepork

morning

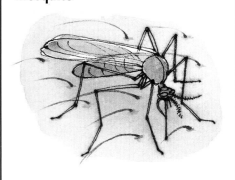

I eat breakfast every **morning**.

mosquito

motel

moth

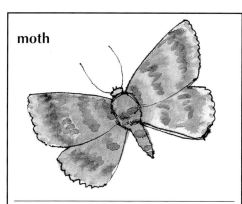

mother

motorbike

mountain

mountain bike

mouse

mouth

mud

mug

I like to drink from a **mug**.

mum

muscle

museum

mushroom

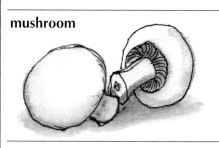

music

musician

mussel

myth

A **myth** is a story about ancient times.

Nn

nail

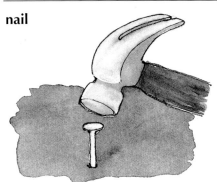

name

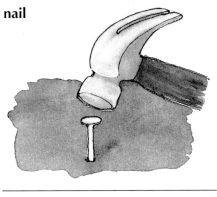

My **name** is Jack.

nature

This is our **nature** table.

naughty

neck
necklace

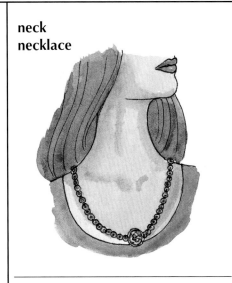

needle

neighbour

nephew

Sam is Joe's **nephew**.

nervous

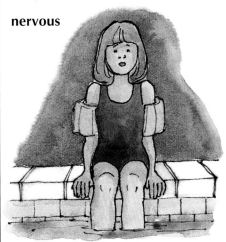

I am **nervous** about learning to swim.

nest

net

new

I have **new** shoes.

news

I watched the **news** last night.

newspaper

niece

Leilani is Eva's **niece**.

night

nightmare

no

noisy

nose

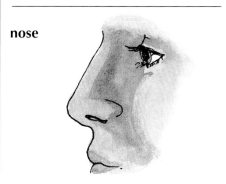

note

Mum wrote a **note** to my teacher.

notice

I saw a **notice** about the school fair.

number

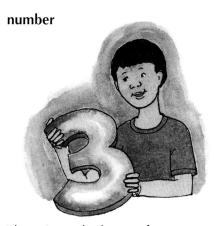

Three is my lucky **number**.

numberplate

nurse

nuts

Oo

oar

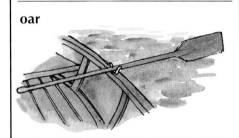

ocean

octopus

oil

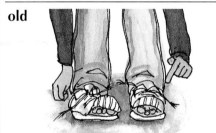

old

on

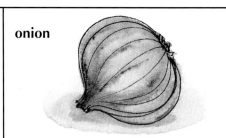

The cat is **on** the television.

onion

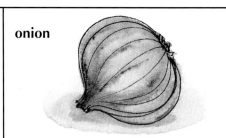

open

The door is **open**.

orange

orange

orchestra

ouch

out

Let that dog **out**.

outside

I like playing **outside**.

oven

over (to the other side)

The ball went **over** the fence.

over (covering)

The paint went all **over** the floor.

owl

oyster

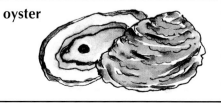

Pp

package

paddle

paddle

paddock

The cows are in the **paddock**.

page

The **page** is torn.

paint

pair

palace

pancake

paper

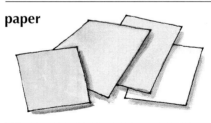

parachute

parakeet

parents

park

We play with our frisbee in the **park**.

parrot

party

P
p

passport

pasta
Spaghetti is my favourite **pasta**.

pastry

path

patient

My mother says, 'Be **patient**!'

patient

pattern

I draw a **pattern** with my felts.

pea

peaceful

peach

peanut

peanut butter

pear

pedestrian crossing

peg

pen

pencil

penguin

people

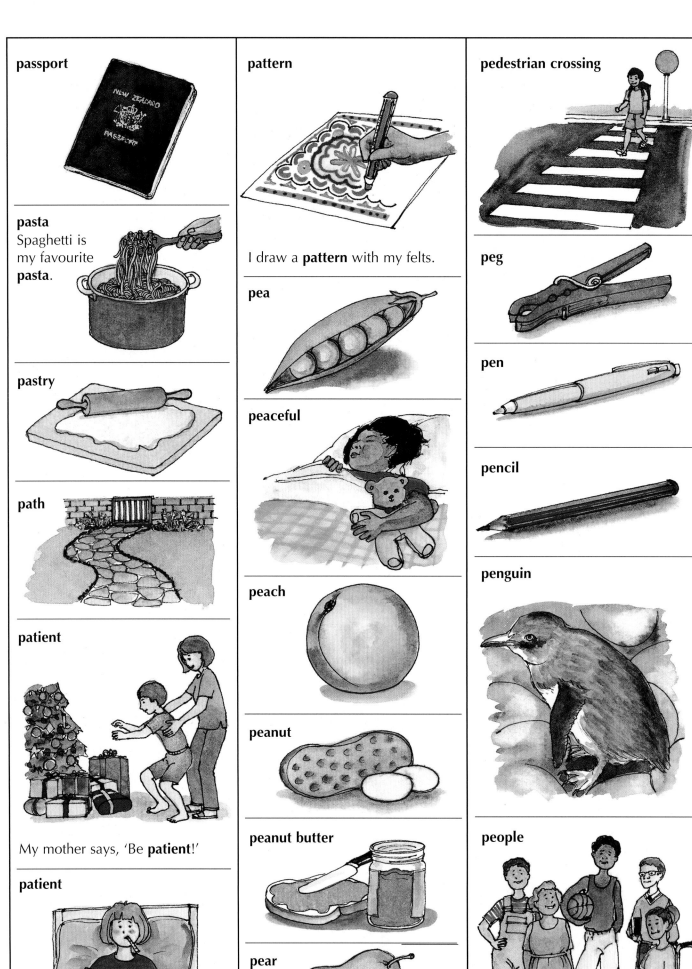

pepper

perfume

pet

petrol
petrol station

phone

photocopier

photograph

photographer

piano

picnic

picture

pie

pig

pigeon

pile
There are
eight books
in this pile.

pill

pillow

pilot

P p

pin

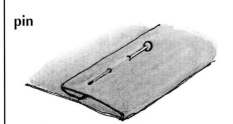

pink

pirate

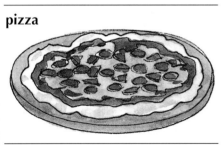

pizza

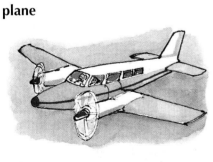

plane

plant

plastic plate

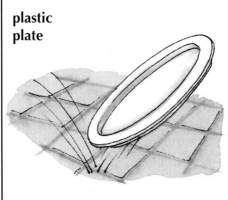

A **plastic plate** won't break.

play playground

please

'**Please** read me another story.'

plug

plum

pocket

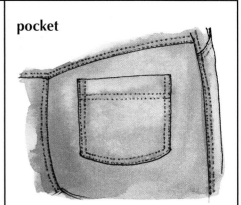

pocket money

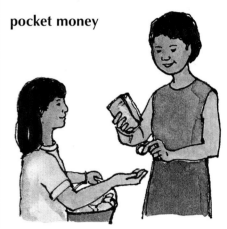

Mum gives me **pocket money** when my jobs are done.

poem

I wrote a **poem** about skateboarding.

polar bear

pole

police officer
My sister is
a **police
officer**.

pollution

pond

pony

pool

popcorn

porch

post

postcard

postie

pot

potato

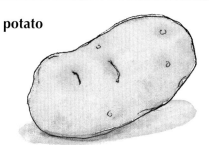

pour

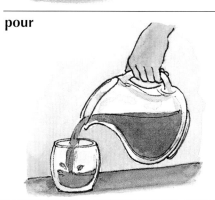

pram

**present
pretty**

The **present** is wrapped in
pretty paper.

price

P p

prince
princess

principal

The **principal** spoke at assembly.

prize
proud

'You won the **prize**. I'm **proud** of you.'

puddle

pull

pumice

Pumice is easy to lift.

pumpkin

puppet

puppy

purple

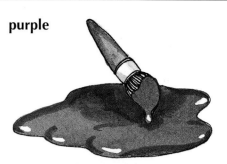

purse

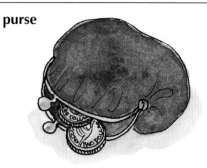

push

pushchair

puzzle

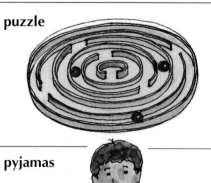

pyjamas

Qq

quarrel

We had a **quarrel** about a shirt.

quarter

queen

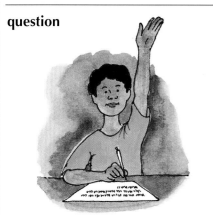

question

I want to ask a **question**.

queue

quickly

I walk **quickly** so I won't be late for school.

quiet

We have to be **quiet** in the library.

quiz

There was a **quiz** about birds in my book.

Rr

rabbit

race

racket

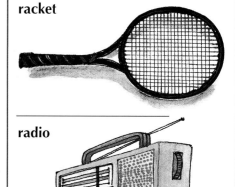

radio

raffle

I sold lots of tickets for the **raffle**.

R r

railway station

rain

rainbow

raincoat

raisins

rake

rat

rattle

read

SCHOOL JOURNAL

red

reed

referee

reflection

refrigerator

remember

I **remember** the teddy I lost.

remote control

reptile

A tuatara is a **reptile**.

rescue

restaurant

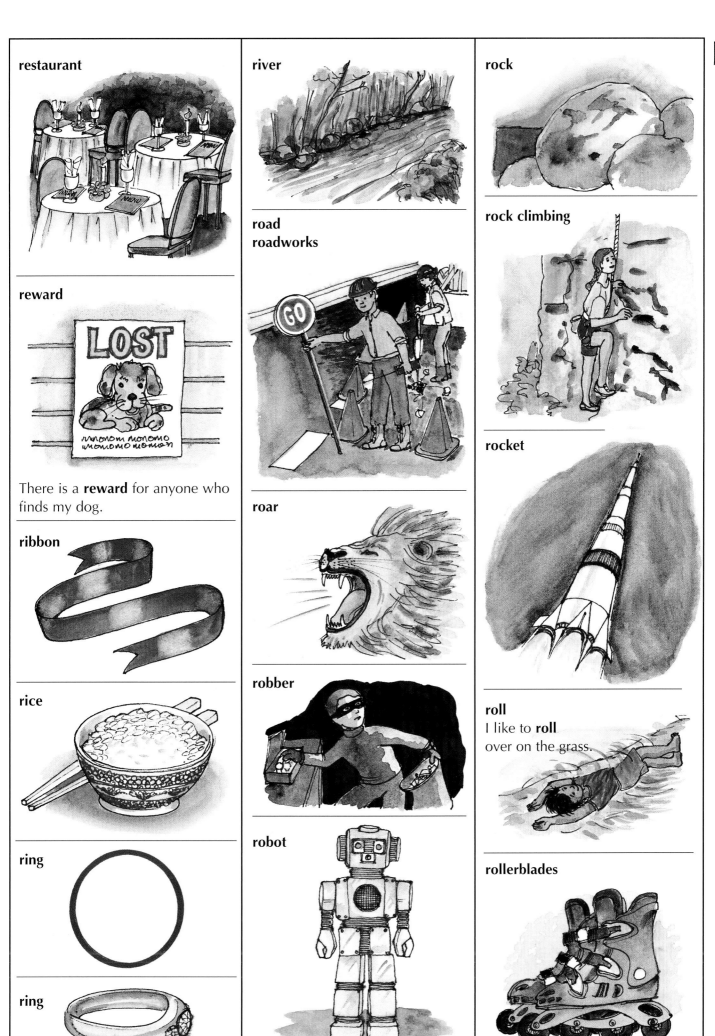

reward

There is a **reward** for anyone who finds my dog.

ribbon

rice

ring

ring

river

road
roadworks

roar

robber

robot

rock

rock climbing

rocket

roll
I like to **roll** over on the grass.

rollerblades

R
r

roof

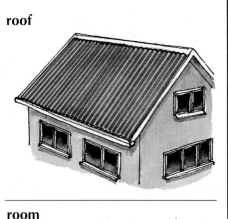

room

This is my **room**.

rooster

root

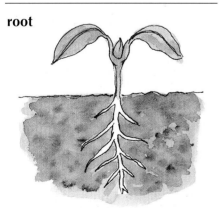

rope

rose

rotten

rough

The road is **rough**.

round

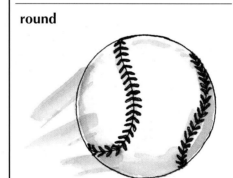

rub

I **rub** my eyes when I am sleepy.

rubber

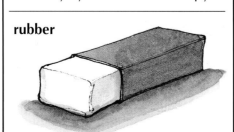

rubbish

rugby

ruler

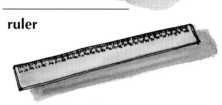

run

runway

Ss

sacred

sad

saddle

sail

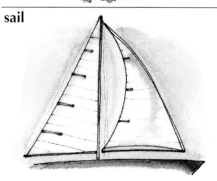

sail
I like to **sail** in my boat.

sailor

salad

salt

sand
sandpit

sandals

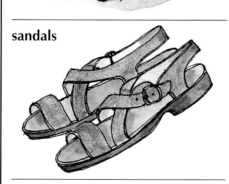

sandfly

sandwich

Santa Claus

sauce

saucepan

sausage

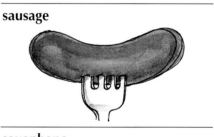

saxophone

S
s

scare

school

schoolbag

science
scientist

scissors

scratch

scream

screen

sea

seafood

seagull

seal

search

I **search** for my soccer boots.

seasick

seat

seatbelt

seaweed

KURA
SCHOOL

see

My new glasses help me to **see**.

seed

seesaw

sell

send

I will **send** a letter to Santa Claus.

sew

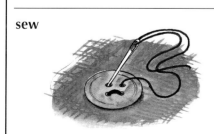

shadow

shake

shake hands

shampoo

shark

shave

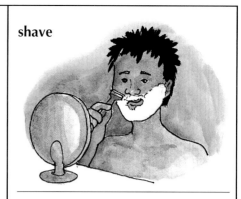

sheep

sheet

I make a hut from a big **sheet**.

shell

shiny

ship

shirt

shiver

shoe
shoelace

shop

shorts

shoulder

shout

shovel

shower

shower

shut

The door is **shut**.

shy

sick

sign

sing
singer

sister

Moana is Rona's little **sister**.

sit

skateboard

skates

skeleton

skin

My **skin** has freckles.

skipping rope

skirt

skull

sky

slam

slap

sleep

sleeping bag

sleeve

slice

slide

slipper

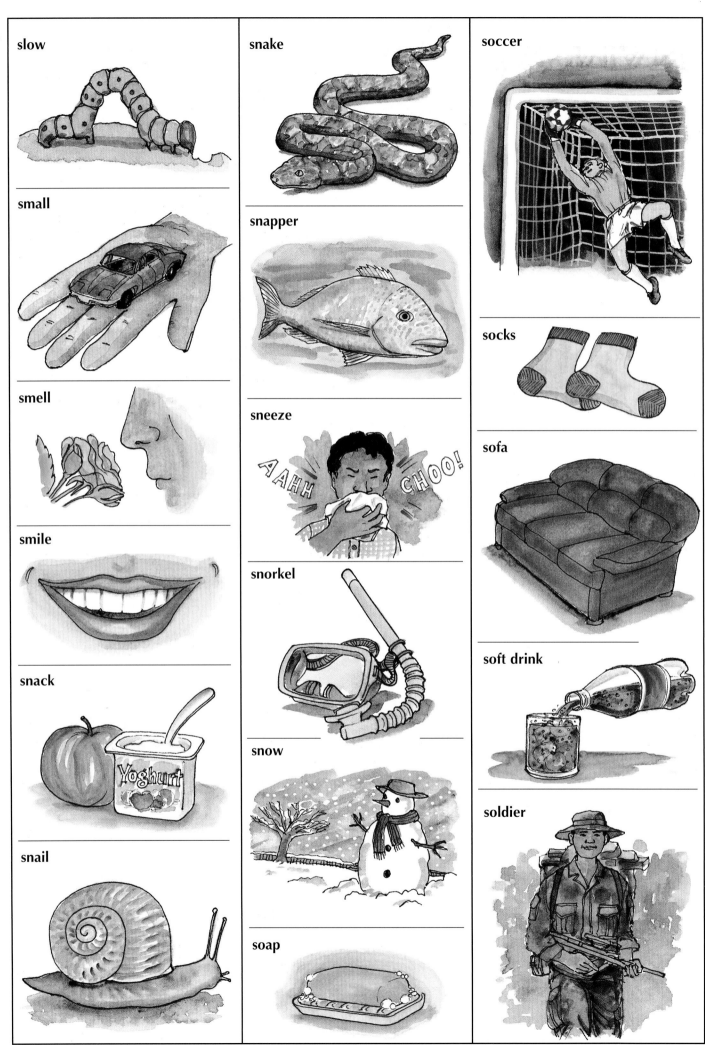

slow

small

smell

smile

snack

snail

snake

snapper

sneeze

A AHH CHOO!

snorkel

snow

soap

soccer

socks

sofa

soft drink

soldier

son

song

I learnt a new **song** today.

sorry

'Oops, **sorry**.'

soup

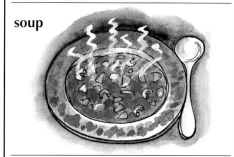

sour

Lemons are **sour**.

space
spaceship

spade

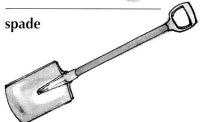

sparrow

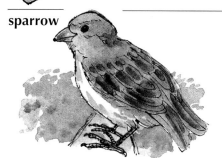

spear

speed
speed camera

speedboat

spelling

We have **spelling** for homework.

spider
spider's web

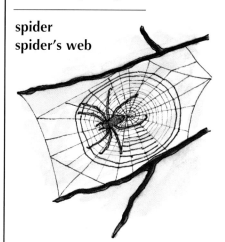

spill

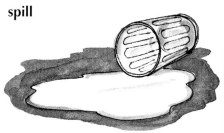

sponge

spoon

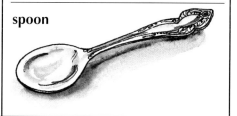

61

sport

I like playing **sport**.

spring

stage

stairs

stamp

stamp

stand

We **stand** up to say good morning to the teacher.

star

starfish

stay

I **stay** in bed when I am sick.

steam

sticking plaster

stingray

stomach

stone

stool

storehouse

storm

story

Grandpa tells me a **story**.

stove

strawberry

stream

street

This is the **street** where I live.

string

stroke

strong

student

submarine

sugar

suit

summer

sun

sunburn

sunglasses

sunscreen

supermarket

surf
The **surf** is rough.

surf
I love to **surf**.

surfboard

surprise

HAPPY BIRTHDAY

swamp

swan

sweatshirt

sweep

sweet

Honey

swim
swimming pool

swing

sword

Tt

table

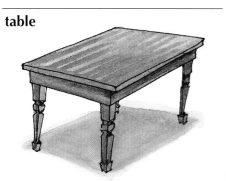

tail

talk

I **talk** to my friend on the telephone.

tall

taste

taxi

tea

teacher

team

teapot

tear

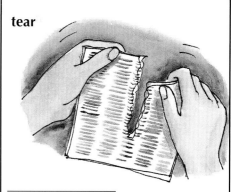

tears

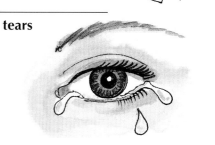

teddy bear

teeth

telephone

television

temper

tennis

tent

thank you

'**Thank you** for having me.'

thick

thief

thin

think

I try to **think** of the answer.

thread

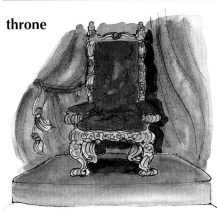

throne

thrush

thumb

thunder
thunderstorm

There was **thunder** and lightning during the **thunderstorm**.

ticket

tickle

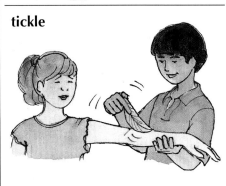

tide

I like to swim when the **tide** is in.

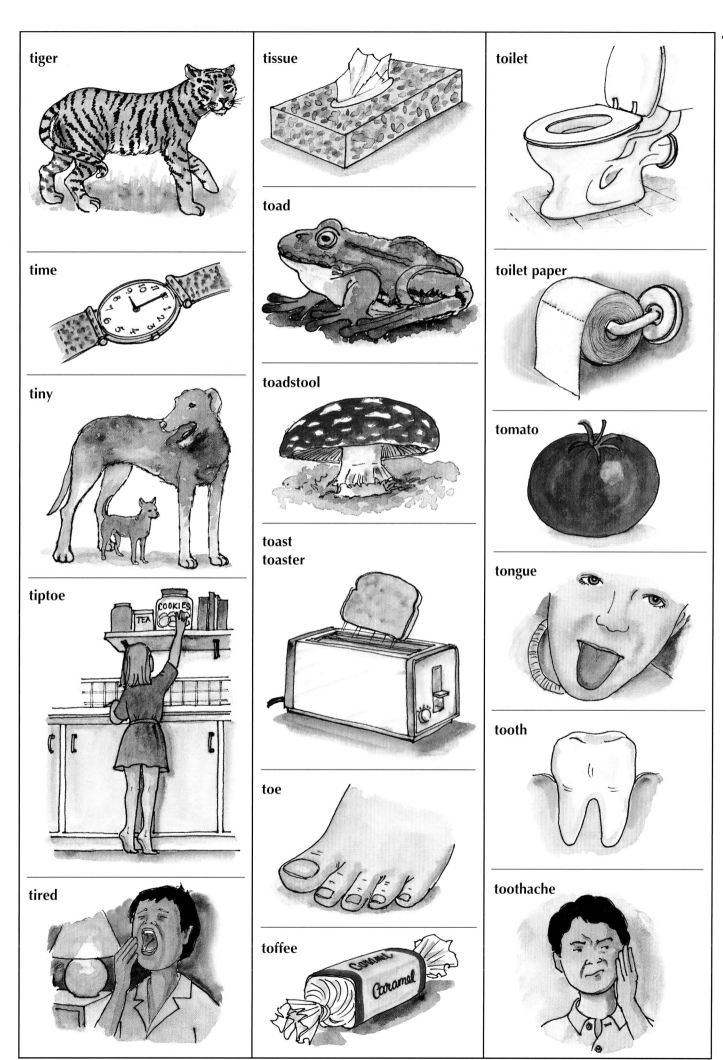

tiger

time

tiny

tiptoe

tired

tissue

toad

toadstool

toast
toaster

toe

toffee

toilet

toilet paper

tomato

tongue

tooth

toothache

toothbrush
toothpaste

topknot

torch

torn

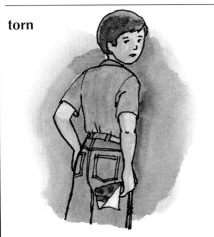

tourist

towel

tower

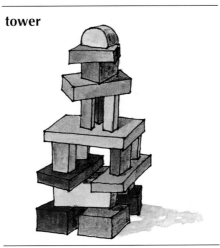

town

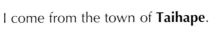

I come from the town of **Taihape**.

toy

track

tracksuit

tractor

traffic jam

traffic lights

train

trampoline

trap

travel

I like to **travel** on the bus.

treasure

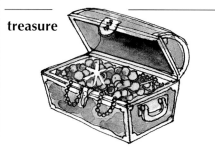

tree

tribe

'My **tribe** is Ngāi Tahu.'

tricycle

trip

'Have a good **trip**.'

trouble

I am having **trouble** with my shoelaces.

trousers

trout

truck

trumpet

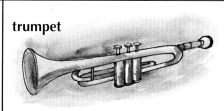

trunk

T-shirt

tunnel

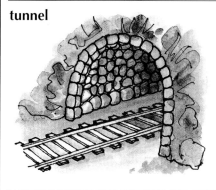

twins

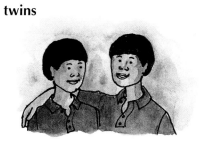

typewriter

Uu

ugly

umbrella

uncle

Mark is Dylan's **uncle**.

under

I hide **under** the table.

underwater

underwear

unhappy

uniform

up

use

I **use** lots of paint.

Vv

vacuum cleaner

van

vase

vegetables

verandah

very

I am **very** strong.

vet

video camera

video tape

vineyard

visitors

volcano

vomit

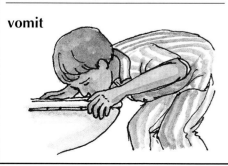

Ww

wade

wag

waist

wait

walk

wall

wall

wallet

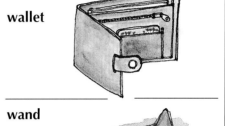

wand

want

'I **want** my dinner.'

wardrobe

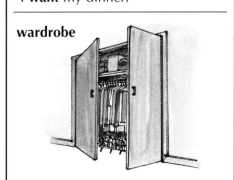

warm

warrior

wash

washing machine

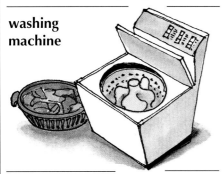

wasp

watch

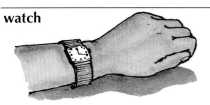

watch

I like to **watch** Dad playing rugby.

water

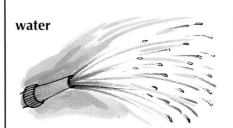

waterfall

watering can

watermelon

water-skiing

wave

wave

weather

In summer the **weather** is hot.

weave

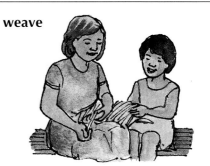

Granny shows me how to **weave**.

wedding

weeds

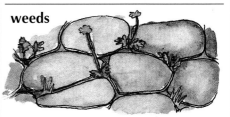

week

A **week** has seven days.

weekend

At the **weekend** I like to play.

welcome

We put on a **welcome** for the new principal.

wet

whale

wharf

wheel

wheelbarrow

wheelchair

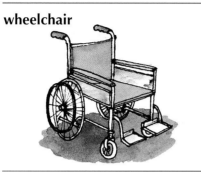

whisper

white

whitebait

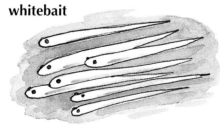

wife

My grown-up brother has a **wife** and a baby.

wildlife

wind

window

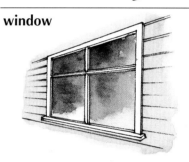

windscreen

windsurfing

wing

73

wink

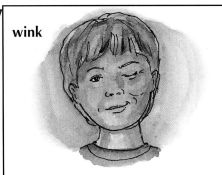

winter

wipe

wish

I **wish** I had a skateboard.

witch
wizard

wolf

woman

wood

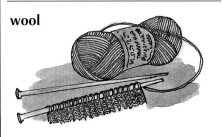

The park bench is made of **wood**.

wool

work

This is hard **work**.

worker

world

worm

worry

I **worry** about my dog. She might be lost.

wrap

I **wrap** up my doll to keep her warm.

write

I **write** a letter to Santa.

Xx

X-ray

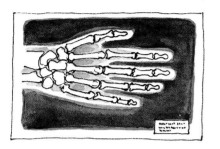

xylophone

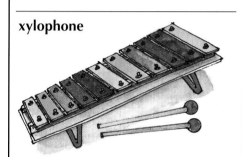

Yy

yacht

yawn

year

There are twelve months in a **year**.

yell

yellow

yes

yoghurt

yolk

Zz

zebra

zebra crossing

zip

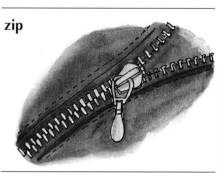

zoo

Days of the week

Monday
Tuesday
Wednesday
Thursday
Friday
Saturday
Sunday

Months of the year

January
February
March
April
May
June

July
August
September
October
November
December

Shapes

circle

square

oval

triangle

rectangle

diamond

Family

adult
auntie
baby
boy
brother
child
children
cousin
dad
daughter

family
father
friend
girl
grandchild
grandfather
grandmother
husband
mother
mum

neighbour
nephew
niece
parents
sister
son
twins
wife
woman

Colours

black

pink

blue

purple

brown

red

green

white

orange

yellow

In the classroom

blackboard
book
bookshelf
chair
chalk
clock
crayon
desk
door
duster
felt-tip pen
glue
mat
paint
paper
pen
pencil
rubber
ruler
scissors
student
teacher
window

Parts of the body

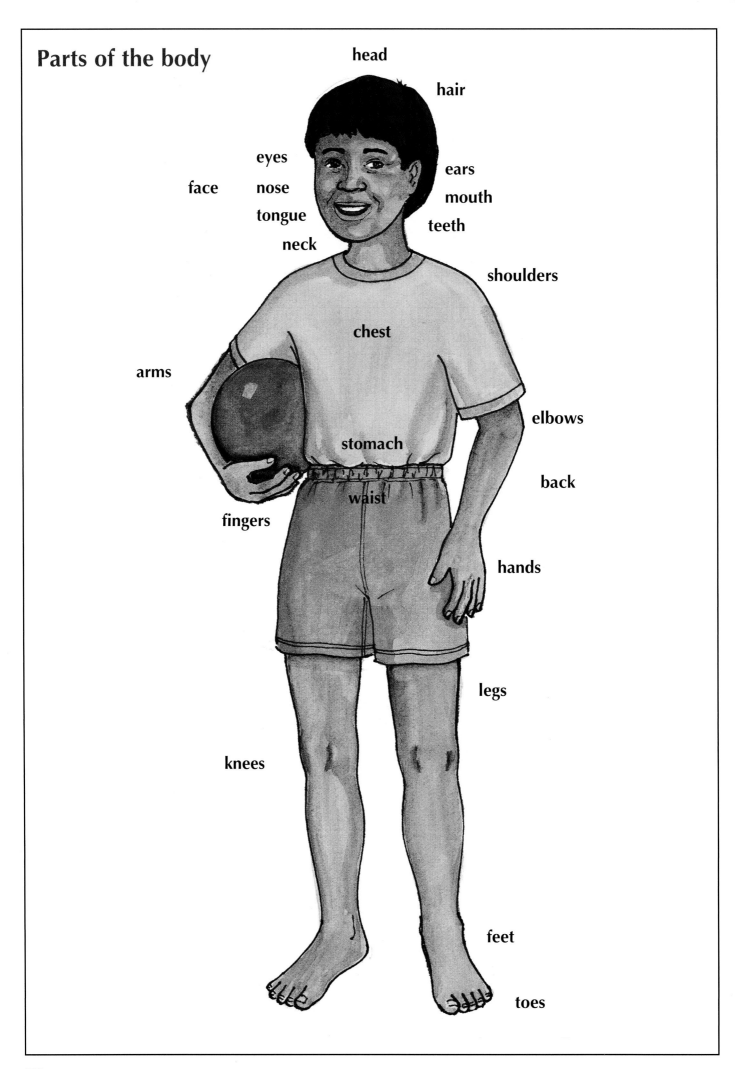

head

hair

eyes

face nose

tongue

neck

ears

mouth

teeth

shoulders

chest

arms

elbows

stomach

back

waist

fingers

hands

legs

knees

feet

toes

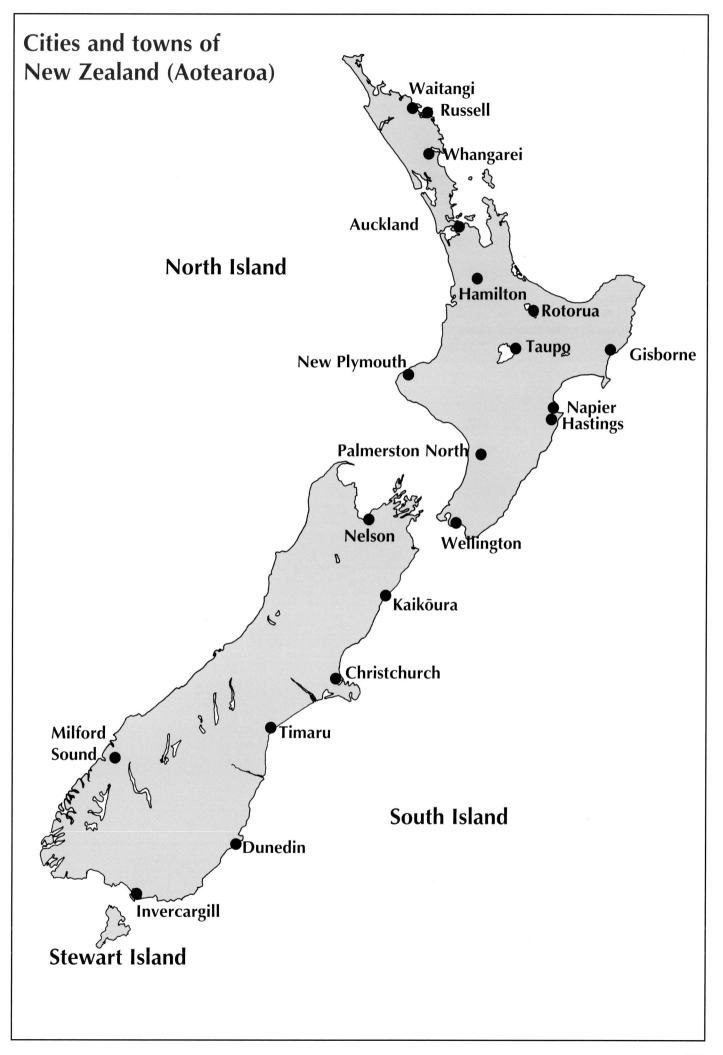

Cities and towns of New Zealand (Aotearoa)

North Island

Waitangi
Russell

Whangarei

Auckland

Hamilton
Rotorua

New Plymouth

Taupo

Gisborne

Napier
Hastings

Palmerston North

Nelson

Wellington

Kaikōura

Christchurch

Milford
Sound

Timaru

South Island

Dunedin

Invercargill

Stewart Island